How to Make a Free Website

Entrepreneur Book Series

M. Usman

Mendon Cottage Books

JD-Biz Publishing

Download Free Books!
http://MendonCottageBooks.com

Disclaimer

The information is this book is provided for informational purposes only. It is not intended to be used and medical advice or a substitute for proper medical treatment by a qualified health care provider. The information is believed to be accurate as presented based on research by the author.

The contents have not been evaluated by the U.S. Food and Drug Administration or any other Government or Health Organization and the contents in this book are not to be used to treat cure or prevent disease.

The author or publisher is not responsible for the use or safety of any diet, procedure, or treatment mentioned in this book. The author or publisher is not responsible for errors or omissions that may exist.

Warning

The Book is for informational purposes only and before taking on any diet, treatment, or medical procedure, it is recommended to consult with your primary health care provider.

Our books are available at
1. Amazon.com
2. Barnes and Noble
3. Itunes
4. Kobo
5. Smashwords
6. Google Play Books

Table of Contents

Preface

Decades ago, it was only big companies that could afford to have websites. Fast forward to today, and an average Joe can have one running in minutes. There are now a lot of companies providing website services, driving costs down on the part of consumers.

Making it even better, some of these companies are generous enough to let you have a website without paying anything. However, it's not everyone who knows how to get a free website. Besides, having a lot of companies that provide the same thing can leave you confused and not knowing which one to choose. Actually, if you are not careful, you can end up paying a high price for something that was advertised as free.

This book will act as your guide to getting a free website. But, as you may know, free usually comes at a cost. So, we will look at the pros and cons of going down this road. I will then show you how easy it can be to set up a free website.

But, since a website will do nothing on its own, I will also give you tips on how you can increase traffic with great content, SEO, and other methods.

I'm sure you will find this book useful, so without wasting any more time, let's get started, because a free website awaits you.

Chapter # 1: Why You Need To Have a Website

When you are new to anything, it is always a good idea to have a goal before you get to action. The same is true when you want to have your own website. In this first chapter, I will introduce you to some of the reasons you may find it necessary to have your own website.

So without wasting any more time, let's get to it:

Everyone is Online – The truth is that more people are now using the internet than ever before. Advancements in computers and mobile devices have made accessing the web much easier. Days of going to the library or contacting a friend to learn about something are long gone. Everyone now knows that if there is something you need, the internet is the place to look for it, no matter where you are. It has even come to a point where you can use Google as a verb.

If you have a business or just want to be discovered, this increasing number of internet users is an opportunity. With your own website, you will be able to reach a lot of people at any time, wherever they are.

Cheap Advertising – Because of the increase in internet users, businesses wanting to advertise on the web can find it cheaper. Putting an ad in the newspaper or TV costs more than it does to have it online, so not only will your marketing messages reach a lot of people, but you will also save some money.

Let Your Skills Be Discovered – For artists all over the world, there is no greater platform to showcase your talent than on your own website. If your visitors like you, they will definitely be converted into fans. With time, you will build your own following. If you do not have a website, you will only be known locally. At the same time, you will not have a lot of fans.

Make Money – It is not easy to make decent money with a website. However, that does not mean you cannot do it. As a matter of fact, there are a lot of people making thousands every month with their websites. But to get to that point, you will need to work hard. Additionally, know that it will take time. One thing you must consider when choosing a free website provider is that it should allow you to monetize your website.

Share Valuable Tips to Change the World – Have you always wanted to have a platform where you could share your ideas with the world? A free website will give you just that. Are you constantly finding hacks that we can all use to improve our lives? Get a free website and share your ideas with the rest of the world.

Share Your Life – You can also have a website just to share your life experiences, as people like to read stories they can relate to.

These are just a few of the reasons people want websites, and there are many other reasons that can make you want to have your own website.

Chapter # 2: Pros and Cons of Free Websites

While there is no money involved in setting up a free website, you may not appreciate some of the drawbacks of going down this road. Perhaps, the saying "there is no such thing as a free lunch" is true after all. Some web developers will even swear that you should never sign up for a free website.

Pros of Free Websites

Here are some of the good things you will get upon registering for a free website:

Free Domain Name – Starting a website requires that you have a domain name. With a free website, you get a name for free. If you were to buy this, you would pay $10 dollars or more per year, depending on the registrar. So if you are low on cash, going with a free website provider would make it possible for you to have your own web presence—at no cost.

Free Storage – Since your website will have documents, pictures, and other contents, you will need some form of storage to keep all this stuff. If you are to host your own website, you will be paying at least $10 per month. So again, you will save on hosting with a free website.

Free Website Builder – If you know nothing about web designing, you will love how fast and easy you can have your own website running in minutes with a free website builder. You will find this so easy to use, as it is usually just drag and drop.

Monetization – You may want to be paid for your efforts. Thankfully, most free website providers will give you a chance to monetize your website in whatever way you want. So, you will make money without spending any in the first place.

Cons of Free Websites

Here are some of the reasons you might want to stay away from free websites:

Unattractive Domain Names – While you will get a free domain name, the truth is that you will not like it. Instead of having www.yourname.com, you will have www.yourname.blogspot.com if using Blogger. Not only is this long, but you will also have trouble passing it to friends during brief encounters.

Limited Storage Space – If you plan to grow your website, you will certainly run out of space with time. So you will have no choice but upgrade at a cost.

You Can Lose Your Website – At any time, the provider can decide to delete your website. Some of the reasons you may face this is if you violate any of its terms or have a lack of activity on your website, etc. If you have to be in this situation, all your work will be lost. If you had any traffic, it will be gone. Actually, this is the number one reason you need to stay away from free website providers.

No Additional Features – If you decide to increase the functionality of your website with plugins, forums, etc., you are out of luck. In fact, you only have two options: upgrade at a cost or stay with what you have.

Lack of Trust – Like it or not, people do not trust free websites. A web address like www.yourname.wordpress.com gives the impression that you are not serious. Likewise, search engines give preference to paid domains over free ones because of lack of trust.

Ads on Your Website – When you register for a free website, you give the provider a license to put advertisements on it. Not only will these distract your readers from concentrating on what you want them to see, but your website will also look untidy.

However, those reasons should not scare you from getting a free website. If you are low on cash or you just want a simple platform to share things that are on your mind, a free website will be adequate. But, if you are running a business, I would advise that you buy a domain name and hosting.

Chapter # 3: Free Website Providers Compared

There are a lot of companies on the internet providing free website services. This is a good thing, since you will have a chance to go for the one that best fulfills your needs. But at the same time, this might also leave you confused and not knowing which company to go for.

Choosing the wrong free website provider can lead to regret later on. You do not want to spend hours creating content on a platform that is not in line with your goals.

So without further ado, here are some websites worth looking at:

Weebly

Weebly is one of the free website service providers that has been around for years. From the time the company began, there have been a lot of improvements in their services. Making Weebly even better, more features are being added.

Below are some things you will need to know about Weebly:

Drag and Drop Website Builder – If you do not know anything about website designing, Weebly's website builder is probably the simplest you can get. You can move everything in any way you want until you are happy with the results.

Easy to Use – Coupled with the nice website builder, you will feel at home even if you have never used Weebly before. Everything is straightforward, so you will know what to do without much research.

Difficult to Migrate – If you ever decide to move your website, you will be out of luck. This could be when you have outgrown Weebly and want to move to another company.

Unattractive Themes – Although you will get a number of themes with the free account, the majority of these are not very attractive and look outdated.

Jimdo

This is one website that will give you a hard time choosing it or Weebly. Jimdo is so much like Weebly in most aspects. However, there are still some big differences between the two that you will need to consider before making your decision.

Easy to Use – Jimdo is easy to use, so you will feel at home even if you have never built a website before. Learning where to find all the tools does not take a lot of time.

A Selection of Themes – Just like with Weebly, you will also have a couple of themes to choose from if you sign up with Jimdo. However, it will take time to find the one that suits your taste.

Ads with Free Plan – With the free plan, Jimdo will place ads on your website. However, almost all free website service providers do this. If you do not want to have adverts on your website, you can easily upgrade to a paying plan.

WordPress

If you are looking for flexibility and customization, there is no better choice than WordPress. As a matter of fact, WordPress powers about 25% of websites on the internet. This shows that people love using this platform. If you are wondering why WordPress is so popular, here are some of the reasons:

Lots of themes to choose from – With WordPress, you have a lot of themes at your fingertips to make your website look the way you want. You will find over 200 free themes to choose from. Making it better, most of these are good looking and responsive.

Versatile and Customizable – In WordPress, you have the power to do just about anything. Whether you want your pages to float or you fancy having pop-ups, you can get it all. There are also lots of plugins that you can add to your website to increase its functionality.

Has a Learning Curve – With such great flexibility comes the need to spend some time learning how to use WordPress. Thankfully, there are a lot of tutorials on the internet you can follow. You will find these in forums, videos, etc. If you ever run into trouble, asking a question on the web will provide you with an answer in no time.

You Pay for Advanced Features – If you want to get the best from WordPress, you will be required to pay a fee.

Wix

This is another website that has expanded in recent years making it worth checking out. Wix also offers a number of features similar to the other websites above.

Customizable – Much like you would expect you will have the chance to move things around until your website looks the way you want it to. Wix also has a number of templates, so you will surely find something you like among the templates they offer.

Easy to Use – If you are a complete beginner to website designing, Wix will not intimidate you with a lot of complicated things to learn. You will find tutorials, including videos, which will accelerate your understanding of this website.

Ads on the Free Plan – As you would expect, Wix puts ads on your website if you are using the free plan.

Blogger

This is a nice platform if you just want to showcase your skills or share the events happening in your life with people. Blogger is from Google so you do not need to create a separate account to start using it.

Easy to Get Started – There is nothing strange about Blogger. Once you are logged in, you will choose a template and a name. Once that is done, you are good to go. You can add texts, images, videos, etc.

Does Not Contain a Lot of Templates – You will have a limited selection of templates with Blogger. Adding to that, it is not very customizable like WordPress.

Make Money – If you want to earn some money, you can monetize your website through a number of strategies.

It is not easy to say which of these websites is the best if you want to have a free website. Only your needs will dictate the one that's suitable for you. So, before you even start researching these websites, have a clear idea of what you would like to do online.

Look and see if the provider you have chosen has plans that will accommodate you in case the free plan is no longer viable.

Chapter # 4: Signing up for a Website

After reviewing your needs and goals, you should be in a position to choose the best provider. Registering with the wrong company will be costly, as it will affect the functionality of your website.

So, once you have made your choice, the next step is to sign up for an account. You will be required to provide your name, email address, and other relevant information.

You will then be presented with a page where you will create a name for your website. There are a couple of things you will need to consider when making this name. Here they are:

Easy to remember – Not everyone will land on your website through a link. Others will type it in their browser after remembering it. So if your URL is not easy to recall, you will lose some readers.

It must be short – Short URLs are easy to remember and reduce the risk of typing mistakes.

Must be meaningful – You cannot just combine some random letters and call it a web address; you need something that has a meaning. Your address should communicate what people will find when they visit it.

Avoid hyphens and numbers – Including those characters will make it difficult to give your web address to others verbally. Additionally, typing or remembering it will also be an issue.

When you are done dealing with the name, you will need to choose a template. Spend time looking at the ones available. Considering that this is a free website, do not expect anything extraordinary.

If you do not like some aspects of your template, you will likely have the option to customize it.

Once that is done, your website will be ready. You can start posting content and sharing your web address with others.

Chapter # 5: Tips for Creating Great Content

If you want to have a popular website, providing your readers with great content is the best strategy you can follow. But, it's not only your readers who will appreciate your hard work; search engines will do the same.

As I said earlier, more people are now using the internet. This has led to an increased demand for content, resulting in more websites being created. The unfortunate consequence is that competition among website owners has stiffened. So, if you want to have a successful website, you will have to work for it.

People get on the web to look for information, which you must provide right then and there. If they do not find what they are looking for, knowing that there are other websites capable of doing what you didn't, they will click the back button and continue their search.

This is the reason you need to create content that will make your readers want to stay. Below are some tips you can follow to achieve that.

Have an attractive heading – Some people create the headline before writing the draft, while others do it after. My advice is to go with whatever you know will work for you. Your focus should be on ending up with a great headline. If it does not tell the reader what he will read in the article, keep rewriting it.

Here is an example of a good and a bad headline:

1. Listen to music when you are working out

2. How to make your exercises easy with music

Assuming that both articles are talking about the same thing, which one would you prefer to read? I would go for the second one.

The first headline does not communicate any benefit to the reader. He will be asking, "What will happen if I listen to music when working out?"

On the contrary, the second one is clear and to the point. Exercising can be hard sometimes, so the reader will know how he can use music to make working out easy.

Writing a great headline takes time. You will need to rewrite until it is perfect.

Add Value – Everyone gets online looking for solutions to their problems. It could be that the computer is not turning on. Or, you could be planning on going for a holiday in Kenya, but are not sure if you will find any good hotels. Whatever the case, as a website owner, your job is to provide that solution.

So, before you publish your content, put yourself in your reader's shoes. Imagine the problems he is going through and decide if your article provides the solutions he is looking for. If it doesn't, rewrite. After all, rewriting creates great content.

Update Regularly – You can write a couple of articles then abandon your website for months. However, your readers will not be pleased with that and you will lose some of them. At the same time, search engines will also punish you with a drop in rankings.

But, this does not mean you should be producing content every day. The website aside, you probably have other things that keep you busy throughout the day. So here is my advice: aim to produce at least two articles per week. If you can do more, that's even better.

Make it Engaging – Just because your readers are desperately looking for an answer does not put them in a position to take anything. If they find your articles to be boring, they will not be patient enough to see your nice conclusion.

Your content should not make them feel like they are a lecturer marking someone's essay.

So now you ask, how can I make my work engaging? You can add stories, videos, pictures, and anything you think will keep them interested. Just make sure that what you include is related to your main topic.

Furthermore, no one likes to read with a dictionary beside them. Remember, this person is at your website to find a solution and not to learn English. So use words they hear every day

Content should be scannable – People do not read online in the same way they read a book. On the web, they scan to find the solution as quickly as possible.

To make your articles scannable, use short paragraphs. Additionally, remove any words that do not add value to what you are trying to say.

If you do that, your points will be clear and the readers will get what they are looking for easily.

Make sure your content is accurate – When doing research, get information from websites you trust, as not everything you will read will be true. If you use inaccurate data, your reputation will be affected. You will lose trust, which will lead to the fall of your website.

Chapter # 6: Introduction to SEO

SEO is an acronym for Search Engine Optimization. In simple language, this means making your website attractive to search engines like Google, Ask, Yahoo, etc. SEO is a broad subject, and so, it is not easy to cover in a single chapter. However, that should not stop you from knowing the basics.

There are mainly two types of SEO which are on-page and off-page.

On-page SEO consists of the use of HTML code, images, texts, and other material in a way that search engines can understand. Mind you, search engines do not see a web page the way you see it. So, as you create your posts, they must follow a format understandable to both human and search robots.

On the other hand, off-page SEO is all about building backlinks which act as votes for you website. The more votes you have, the bigger the chance of making it in the first pages of search results.

There are a lot of things that are used to determine the rank of your website. One of these is your keywords (the words people type in the search bar of a web browser when looking for something).

For example, "best budget laptops" is a keyword. If a lot of people are searching for laptops with it, using it on your website will increase your traffic. Keywords must be placed strategically all over your website. Search engines will use this to tell what the page is all about.

The Importance of SEO

SEO is an important part of any website. Here are some of the reasons to use it:

It improves your rankings – It is not common to click through pages of search results. If you do not find what you are looking for on the first page, you will likely search using another keyword. So if your website is optimized, you will increase your chances of making it to the first page. This will lead to an increase in traffic.

Cost effective – Advertising a website on the internet is not cheap. But if you use SEO, you will save because you will get targeted traffic without spending any money on advertising.

Improves your website's friendliness – In your effort to please search engines, your website will undergo a transformation that will improve how your visitors enjoy it.

How to Do Basic SEO

Mastering SEO will take time. As a matter of fact, if you have money and are serious about being successful, you may need to hire an SEO specialist. However, that should not stop you from learning a thing or two about the subject.

Use Keywords Strategically – Finding the right keywords take time. You may pay for a keyword research tool or use one of the free options like Google's keyword research tool. You should look for keywords that have a lot of traffic and low competition. If you do that, you will get more traffic and it will be easy for your website to rank higher in search results.

For every article, have at least one keyword. This must be included in the title. Additionally, you should have it in the first and last paragraphs. You can then include it anywhere you want in the article. Just make sure you do not use it for more than 2%. Otherwise, you will be penalized for what is known as keyword stuffing.

Keywords must also be placed in your URL.

Add keywords to images – If you want to have images in your post, make sure that they are related to the topic. They must have a description that best describes what the picture is about, as search engines do not see, but rather read the information you provide.

Apart from that, your images must not be big in size. Otherwise, they will take ages to load which is something search engines do not like.

Have inbound links – Once you have written a number of posts on your website, you should take time to link them to one another. This will help search engine spiders when crawling your website. Just make sure that what you are linking to is relevant.

Link to external websites – If you used information from other websites in your posts, it is important to link to those external sources. You will help the search engines understand what your post is all about.

Update Regularly – As I said in the previous chapter, search engines love websites that are updated regularly. Content is king, so if you have a lot of it, you will see your website rise in search results. However, make sure that the content is great.

Make it easy to navigate – If people find your website hard to navigate, they will certainly leave right away. Not only will you lose readers, but you will also be punished by search engines for having a high bounce rate.

Don't buy links – You may be tempted to buy links in an effort to improve your standings. But this is a bad practice and you will be punished for it. If you want to build links, do it the traditional way. It will take time and a lot of work, but it is worth all the work in the end.

Chapter # 7: How to Promote Your Website

If you do not promote your website, no one will discover it. In fact, you will be its only reader. To avoid such a scenario from happening, you must use the right promotional strategies.

Unfortunately, this topic is not the prettiest part of having a website. It's a lot of work and it takes time.

Some of the strategies you can use have already been discussed in previous chapters which are creating great content and SEO. However, these two will not give you the results you want on their own. So, here are other methods you can follow:

Guest blogging – When you do it right, this can improve traffic to your website. Guest blogging is the act of writing articles for other websites for free. In exchange, your address is placed in the article. As you can see, this increases the number of your backlinks.

At the same time, if the article is great, people who read it will likely follow you to your website.

However, there are a couple of things you must ensure before you start guest blogging. Firstly, you should have some great articles on your website. Otherwise, you will have a difficult time securing a guest blogging opportunity.

Secondly, you should go for websites that have authority. By doing this, you will get quality backlinks which will improve your ranking.

Social Media – Almost everyone uses social media sites. These include Facebook, Twitter, Pinterest, etc. These websites give you a platform to engage with your readers in a lot of ways. As a matter of fact, with the right social media strategy, you can get more traffic from these sites than from search engines.

However, considering that the web has a lot of social networking sites, you will need to choose only those you know will help fulfill your goals. So, start with a research of the networking sites your readers use. Once you are done with that, come up with content that will get their attention.

Use Forums – Although forums are not as popular as they were, they can still be used to promote your website. Make sure that you only join those that are in line with your topic.

And, before you start promoting your website, take time to become a trusted member of the community. Respond to people's answers without any reference to your website. Once you have established trust, add a link to your site now and then. Do not over do it because you may be labeled a spammer, which will result in the closure of your account.

Tell it to friends – Although you will not get a lot of hits from your friends, the presence can help popularize your website when it is in its infancy.

Share free stuff – Writing ebooks and sharing them for free on your website is another common strategy of increasing traffic.

Conclusion

I believe you now know how easy it can be to create a free website. The most important thing is to choose a provider that has what you need. If you do that, what follows will go smoothly.

However, having a website online is just a part of the story. You will have to keep adding great content, which makes people come back for more. Likewise, search engines will send you more traffic which will lead to the growth of your website.

Unfortunately, you only get so much for free. An increase in visitors will give birth to needs that your free plan does not cater to. If the provider you choose makes it easy to upgrade, then good for you, as migrating a website is a pain in the you-know-what.

If you predict that your website will expand soon after being launched, then it is advisable to buy a domain name and hosting now, rather than waste time with free plans. You will only save yourself from the hassle that is associated with migrating.

The good thing is that domain names and hosting have fallen in price, making it possible for anyone to have a paid website without breaking the bank.

Thank you again for reading, and good luck!

References

Image Links

https://pixabay.com/en/blowing-communication-computer-15795/

https://pixabay.com/en/office-freelancer-computer-business-625893/

https://pixabay.com/en/beautiful-business-computer-female-15704/

https://pixabay.com/en/wordpress-hand-logo-589121/

https://pixabay.com/en/office-home-office-creative-apple-581131/

https://pixabay.com/en/mac-freelancer-macintosh-macbook-459196/

https://pixabay.com/en/search-engine-optimization-seo-586422/

https://pixabay.com/en/mac-freelancer-macintosh-macbook-459196/

Author Bio

Muhammad Usman is a distinguished medical graduate of Allama Iqbal medical college (AIMC). He is a professional writer who has been in the field for more than 4 years. During this time he has produced 10,000+ articles, blogs, and eBooks on various niches related to diseases, health, fitness, nutrition, and well-being. He is a regular contributor to several journals related to medicine and surgery. He is the editor of several journals and newspapers.

Download Free Books!
http://MendonCottageBooks.com

Check out some of the other JD-Biz Publishing books

Gardening Series on Amazon

Amazing Animal Book Series

Learn To Draw Series

How to Build and Plan Books

Entrepreneur Book Series

Our books are available at

1. Amazon.com

2. Barnes and Noble

3. Itunes

4. Kobo

5. Smashwords

6. Google Play Books

Download Free Books!
http://MendonCottageBooks.com

Publisher

JD-Biz Corp

P O Box 374

Mendon, Utah 84325

http://www.jd-biz.com/